Greek Myths

ODYSSEUS

JILL DUDLEY

PUT IT IN YOUR POCKET SERIES
ORPINGTON PUBLISHERS

Published by
Orpington Publishers

Cover design and origination by
Creeds, Bridport, Dorset
01308 423411

Printed and bound in the UK by
Creeds

© Jill Dudley 2016

ISBN: 978-0-9934890-3-7

ODYSSEUS

Odysseus was described by Homer as 'cunning' and 'resourceful'. He was quick-thinking, and a man who spoke with authority. He was also able to endure great hardship when the odds were stacked against him. In short, he was a James Bond survivor.

This great Greek hero was the only son and heir of King Laertes of Ithaka. He was married to Penelope, and they too had one only son named Telemachus who was born at the start of the Trojan War.

Odysseus was a favourite of the goddess Athena who frequently intervened to give him divine guidance. It was Odysseus who, after nine years of war, masterminded the idea of the Wooden Horse* which tricked the Trojans into thinking it was a gift for Athena to appease her for his earlier daring theft of her ancient wooden image, the *palladium*. The *palladium* was highly valued by the Trojans as it was believed to have fallen from heaven, and the defence of the city depended on it; its disappearance, Odysseus knew, would gravely undermine Trojan morale.

The Wooden Horse was left on the Trojan plain in full view of the city. Inside it were hidden thirty or so of the most courageous heroes of the Greek army. The Trojans were tricked into supposing the war was over because the Greeks burned their huts and sailed away. In fact, the fleet was hiding behind the nearby island of Tenedos and, under cover of darkness, the ships sailed back, and the Wooden Horse warriors were released by a spy who had managed to bluff his way into the city. They swiftly killed the guards, opened the gates in the defence walls and the Greek soldiers swept in. So began the total destruction of the city.

It was after the sacking of Troy, when on his homeward journey, described by Homer in his epic poem the *Odyssey*, that Odysseus showed his greatest courage and endurance. After the ten-year Trojan War, it would be another ten years before he reached home due to the anger of Poseidon, god of the sea.

When Odysseus and his ships arrived in the land of the Cyclopes, one-eyed monsters whose occupation was sheep farming, Polyphemus (Poseidon's son by a sea-nymph) captured Odysseus and the crew of his ship, and imprisoned them in his cave along with his flock of woolly sheep which he brought in for the night. He placed a great rock before the mouth of the cave so there could be no escape. When he asked Odysseus his name, Odysseus replied 'Nobody'. That night for his supper, to their great horror, Polyphemus seized two of Odysseus' companions *'...and slapped them, like killing puppies against the ground...and like a lion reared in the hills, without leaving anything, ate them, entrails, flesh and...bones alike...'* (Odyssey 9:289-293)

The next evening Polyphemus again killed and ate two of his men. But by now Odysseus had devised a plan. He gave his captor a bowlful of his best wine which so pleased him, that he gulped down great quantities of it till he '...*slumped away and fell on his back, and lay there with his thick neck crooked over on one side, and sleep who subdues all came on and captured him, and the wine gurgled up from his gullet with gobs of human meat...*' (Odyssey 9:371-374)

As soon as this son of Poseidon had passed out, Odysseus sharpened the end of an olive-wood stake and put it in the fire till it glowed red-hot. He and his men then drove it into Polyphemus' one eye, turning it and grinding it in '*...and the blood boiled around the hot point...and the fire made the roots of his eye crackle...*' (Odyssey 9:388,390)

The Cyclops shrieked and, when his fellow Cyclopes called out who was killing him, he replied 'Nobody', so they ignored him. In the morning Polyphemus fumbled about blindly; he removed the rock from the mouth of the cave to let out his sheep, and Odysseus and his men escaped by clinging to the underside of the largest of them.

After surviving that traumatic ordeal, Odysseus and his companions next arrived at the island of Aeolia ruled by Aeolus, lord of the winds. He entertained them well, and they stayed with him for a month. When Odysseus asked about sailing home, his host was very helpful and gave him a leather bag in which he had imprisoned all the winds. Aeolus tied the mouth of the bag with a silver string so not a breath of the wrong wind should escape to slow down his journey; only the west wind was allowed to go free to help them sail back to Ithaka. The leather bag of contrary winds was stowed safely away in Odysseus' ship, and for ten days they made good progress. But while Odysseus was asleep, his men, thinking that Aeolus had given Odysseus a bag full of gold and silver, were tempted to take a look. As soon as the silver string was untied the wild winds burst out.

In no time they found themselves blown back to Aeolia where Aeolus was aggrieved to see them again. He believed that their return showed they had displeased the gods. He sent them on their way once more, and they came to the land of the Laestrygones, man-eating giants. There they were attacked by these monsters who threw missiles down on them from the cliffs.

Managing to escape from them, they then arrived at the island of Aeaea. There the enchantress Circe lived. Immediately she turned his men into swine and drove them into styes and fed them acorns. Odysseus, with the help of the god Hermes who was disguised as a young man, was kept immune from her spells by being given a special magic herb. Hermes told Odysseus that he must draw his sword on Circe, make her swear an oath to reverse her witchcraft over his companions, and turn them back into men, then assist them on their homeward journey. Hermes added that if Circe invited him to her bed, he must not refuse her. Odysseus obeyed Hermes' instructons, and they were treated with such kindness by her that a whole year passed before Odysseus could be persuaded by his men to leave her. He then reminded her of the oath she had sworn, and she told him that before he could get home, he must first consult the shade of Tiresias down in Hades, and she gave him instructions how to summon up the souls of the dead.

As well as speaking to Tiresias who advised him on the best way to journey home, he met the shades of a number of his fellow warriors who had died on the battlefield. He also spoke to his mother Anticlea who had died in his absence. She confirmed what Tiresias had already told him that his wife Penelope was being pestered daily by many suitors hoping to marry her.

After his mournful visit to Hades, Odysseus faced more challenges. He had to pass the island where the Sirens lived, strange women whose singing was so beautiful it enticed mariners to their certain deaths. To avoid such a disaster, Odysseus got his men to plug their ears with beeswax, and instructed them to lash him to the mast and to tighten his bonds if he began to struggle to get free.

Having successfully accomplished this hazardous trip past the Siren voices, Odysseus was next confronted with the even more perilous task of navigating the straits between Scylla and Charybdis. Charybdis threatened to suck his ship down into her deadly whirlpool, while Scylla was a monster with six heads, each having a mouth with three rows of teeth, and a waist around which were dogs' heads which bayed ravenously to be fed.

Odysseus only managed to escape the threat from Charybdis by sailing closer to Scylla at the cost of the lives of six men. He described the incident: *'...and when I turned to look...I saw their feet and hands from below, already lifted high above me, and they cried out to me and called me by name, the last time they ever did it...'* (Odyssey 9:247-250)

He and his men next found themselves on the island of Thrinacia where adverse winds kept them for a month. The shade of Tiresias had warned him not to touch the cattle of Helios there, and he in his turn had forbidden his men to do so. But they were starving, and while Odysseus slept, they killed the sacred cattle. After feasting on the meat for nearly a week, they sailed away but, almost immediately Zeus, on the request of Helios, sent a horrific storm which smashed the boat to smithereens, drowning all his men. He himself was able to cling to the mast and keel which he lashed together, but was swept back to the fearful Charybdis. '...*I came to the sea rock of Scylla, and dreaded Charybdis. At this time Charybdis sucked down the sea's salt water, but I reached high to the air above me, to where the tall fig tree grew, and caught hold of it and clung like a bat...I hung on, waiting for her to vomit the keel and mast back up again...Then I let go my hold with hands and feet, and dropped off...*' (Odyssey 12:430-433, 437-438,442) By paddling frantically with his hands he managed to get clear of her.

Nine days later he was washed up on Oxygia, an island where the beautiful enchantress Calypso had her cavern. '...*She was singing inside the cave with a sweet voice as she went up and down the loom and wove with a golden shuttle. There was a growth of grove around the cavern, flourishing alder was there, and the black poplar, and fragrant cypress, and there were birds with spreading wings who made their nests in it, little owls, and hawks...and right about the hollow cavern extended a flourishing growth of vine that ripened with grape clusters...*' (Odyssey 5:61-69)

Odysseus was bewitched by Calypso and might have stayed indefinitely had Athena, after seven years, not intervened. She pleaded with Zeus to help Odysseus to escape Calypso's clutches. The messenger god Hermes was sent to reason with her, and reluctantly she helped build a raft on which to help him sail away. But Poseidon returned from a seventeen day visit to Ethiopia and, discovering Odysseus on his way home on a raft, sent down a violent storm. He was still angry with him for blinding his son Polyphemus. A sea-goddess disguised as a gannet saved his life by giving him a veil to wrap around himself which prevented him from drowning.

Eventually he was swept up on the shores of Scheria (thought to be Corfu) where he was found by the king's daughter Nausicaa and taken to the palace. After hearing the story of his adventures at a banquet that evening, the kindly King Alcinous arranged for a boat and crew to take him back to Ithaka the next day.

Once back on his own rocky island of Ithaka, Athena in her wisdom disguised him as an elderly beggar so he could go up to his palace unrecognized; he would then be able to see for himself the hundred or more suitors who came daily to eat his food and drink his wine.

Only his old dog Argos recognized him beneath his disguise and, as he approached the gates to the palace, the poor neglected animal ...*wagged his tail, and laid both his ears back; only he now no longer had the strength to move any closer to his master, who, watching him from a distance...secretly wiped a tear away...and...the doom of dark death now closed over the dog, Argos...* (Odyssey 17:302-326)

Odysseus' wife Penelope had for long delayed coming to any decision regarding which suitor she would marry, saying she would only decide when she had finished weaving a shroud for her father-in-law. This she was seen doing by day, but secretly at night she unravelled what she had done. Some years had now passed and she knew she could not persist any longer with this ruse.

Seeing this elderly beggar at the palace hoping for food, the suitors taunted him, and one threw a missile at his head. Odysseus accepted the treatment quietly. Penelope was informed that the beggar claimed to have news of Odysseus, and she asked that he should be brought to her. She treated him kindly as a man who had fallen on hard times. He said he was from Crete and had fought with Odysseus in the Trojan War, and that he knew Odysseus was still alive, and would soon be home.

The goddess Athena put it into Penelope's mind to set a test for the suitors. She announced that she would marry whichever one of them was able to string a bow that had once belonged to Odysseus, and then fire an arrow through the hole in twelve axe-heads lined up in a row.

The next day the contest was held, and a great banquet was arranged for the occasion. With the feast over, the bow was fetched and the axe-heads set up. The suitors all tried to string the bow which required great strength, but each one failed. The 'vagrant' asked to be allowed to try. The suitors, who were about to learn a hard lesson for their insolence, poured scorn on him.

Odysseus took the bow, grasped it firmly, strung it with comparative ease and, to the amazement of the suitors, took aim and fired the arrow through each of the twelve axe-heads. They had not long to be amazed because following on from that, Odysseus and his faithful servants fired arrows at the suitors, killing them all in turn until there was a pile of corpses. After the bodies had been carried outside, and the hall thoroughly cleansed, Odysseus' old nurse Euryclea went up to Penelope to tell her the good news ...*The old woman, laughing loudly, went to the upper chamber to tell her mistress that her beloved husband was inside the house...* (Odyssey 23:1-3) But Penelope was cautious, fearful that the gods were playing a trick. She came down and saw the beggar and took a seat a little apart from him. ...*She sat a long time in silence, and her heart was wondering. Sometimes she would look at him, with her eyes full upon him, and again would fail to know him in the foul clothing he wore...* (Odyssey 23:93-96)

Odysseus instinctively knew what was needed. He called for music and dancing, and for everyone to put on their finest garments. The goddess Athena played her part and, after Odysseus had bathed and dressed, she removed from him all traces of the elderly vagrant in rags, and made him appear like a god.

Even then, it was not until he spoke to Penelope of things which only the two of them could possibly know, that Penelope dared believe it really was him. And so the great warrior king, after ten years of warfare, and ten more of struggle and adversity on his journey home from Troy, found himself back at last in the arms of his beloved wife – 'circumspect Penelope', as Homer described her.

* Denotes a separate booklet on the subject.

GLOSSARY OF GODS AND HEROES

AEOLUS – Ruler of Aeolia, and lord of the winds.

ALCINOUS – King of the Phaeacians, father of Nausicaa.

ANTICLEA – Wife of King Laertes, and mother of Odysseus.

ATHENA – Daughter of Zeus. She was born mature and fully armed from his head. She was goddess of handicraft, and protectress of many cities, especially Athens. She was a great supporter of Odysseus, and often intervened on his behalf.

CALYPSO – A minor goddess, daughter of Atlas, and an enchantress.

CHARYBDIS – A dangerous whirlpool.

CIRCE – An enchantress, and daughter of Helios.

CYCLOPES – One-eyed giants.

EURYCLEA – Odysseus' old nurse.

HADES – God of the underworld.

HELIOS – The sun.

HERMES – Son of Zeus and the mortal woman Maia. He was his father's messenger, and also conducted the souls of the dead down to Hades.

LAERTES – Father of Odysseus.

MENELAUS – King of Sparta and husband of Helen.

NAUSICAA – Daughter of King Alcinous of the Phaeacians.

NESTOR – King of Pylos.

PENELOPE – Wife of Odysseus.

POLYPHEMUS – A Cyclops, son of Poseidon and a sea-nymph.

POSEIDON – God of the sea as well as of earthquakes and horses.

SCYLLA – A sea-monster with six heads and around her waist a string of ravenous barking dogs.

SIRENS – The Siren Voices whose singing lured mariners to their death.

TELEMACHUS – Son of Odysseus and Penelope.

TIRESIAS – A Theban seer.

ZEUS – Supreme god of the ancient world.

ACKNOWLEDGEMENT

Grateful acknowledgement to Richmond Lattimore's translation of
The Odyssey by Homer, Harper Perennial Modern Classics edition, published 2007.

MORE FROM THE
PUT IT IN YOUR POCKET SERIES

GREEK ISLAND MYTHS

ALL YOU NEED TO KNOW ABOUT
THE ISLAND'S MYTHS, LEGENDS
AND ITS GODS

CHIOS

CRETE

KOS

NAXOS

RHODES

SANTORINI

ALSO BY JILL DUDLEY

YE GODS! (TRAVELS IN GREECE)

YE GODS! II (MORE TRAVELS IN GREECE)

LAP OF THE GODS (TRAVELS IN CRETE
AND THE AEGEAN ISLANDS)